What happens next?

INFORMATION FOR KIDS ABOUT SEPARATION AND DIVORCE

Table of Contents

Note to parents and guardians 5

Introduction 6

CHAPTER ONE:
Everything is changing   8

The family 9

Farah's story 11

CHAPTER TWO:
Coming up with a plan for you   14

Dad gives Randy a tough time 15

What's mediation? 16

Mom leaves dad; everyone gets help 17

CHAPTER THREE:
Decisions, decisions, decisions   18

Greta's in the middle 19

Marie is not just a babysitter 20

"Our feet are sore!" agree the twins 23

CHAPTER FOUR:
Living in two homes   24

Jacques gets used to it 25

When things work out 27

CHAPTER FIVE:
What happens if there is violence?   28

Tommy's family finds shelter 29

CHAPTER SIX:
Blended families and extended families,
foster families and guardianship   32

Melody's story 33

Ron's grandmother takes charge 34

CHAPTER SEVEN:
When one parent moves far away   36

Jordan's mom Kristy wants to move 37

CHAPTER EIGHT:
Nothing is perfect, but...   40

Pearl's birthday present 41

APPENDICES

1. Activities 42

2. More information 58

3. Explanation of terms 59

Note to parents and guardians

This booklet has two purposes. First, it's meant to help children between nine and twelve years old learn some basic facts about family law and give them an idea of the processes that parents may go through when they split up.

Second, it's meant to help children realize that it's normal for them to have an emotional response to the divorce of their parents. The booklet encourages children to think about voicing their concerns to someone they trust — like parents, grandparents, uncles and aunts or family friends, neighbours or someone from their church, synagogue or mosque.

The language and activities in the booklet are designed for children. However, some children may need help reading the booklet.

Other children may want help. They may want an adult they trust to work through the booklet with them — helping them understand key legal concepts and cope with any sense of loss, anger, confusion or anxiety.

The booklet is designed to be read all the way through or just in chapters. Kids can read only the chapters that interest them. They can always go back to other chapters later if they need to.

Because this is a booklet for children, a lot of technical, legal information has been left out. This booklet only provides very general information because family law is a complex subject and some aspects of family law are different in each Canadian province and territory.

A section listing more sources of information and sources of support has been included near the end of the booklet. This list will help kids and adults find ways to get more information.

Introduction

So... your parents have decided to split up. You probably have a lot of questions, like "What does this mean for me?" and "Do I still have a family?" or "Will I always feel this bad?" or "Will anyone listen to me?"

You're not alone. A lot of other kids have wondered the same things.

"**Divorce is about the law and about feelings**".

Some of the information in this booklet is about the **law*** and the **legal system***.

In Canada, family law is a bit different in each province and territory. That's why this booklet can only cover very general information. Look at the back of this booklet for books and websites that will give you more information. Or, ask someone close to you to help you get the answers you need. The legal words are explained at the end of the booklet.

The rest of the information in the booklet is about thoughts and feelings. The short stories will show you what other kids have been through when their parents split up. These stories won't be the same as the story of your own family because every family is different. But, they may help you figure out your own feelings.

Near the end of the booklet are some activities that you can try doing. Find the ones you think would help you. Try to have some fun while you do them.

There is a lot of information in this booklet. If you don't know where to start, try asking someone you trust (your parents, a relative or even a teacher) to read it with you.

You can take your time reading this booklet and you can take your time thinking about it. If you want, you can read part of it now, and save the rest for later. It's up to you.

You may find parts of the booklet upsetting. Usually, it's a good idea to talk to someone you trust when things worry or upset you. But, you may decide it wouldn't be a good idea for you to do that right now. You can talk to someone later, but only if you want to.

REMEMBER...

- Your family has changed, but you're still part of a family.
- You didn't cause your parents to split up.
- You don't have to choose between your parents just because they don't live together.
- It's normal to be sad or even angry after your parents split up.
- Find someone you trust to talk to.
- You are not alone; many children go through this.
- You may have friends whose parents have split up. Your experience won't be exactly the same as theirs because there's no-one else quite like you. You are unique. Your thoughts and feelings are important.
- And remember, your voice counts!

Chapter One
Everything is changing

The family

Families are different all over the world. They come in a variety of sizes and shapes. No matter what your family looks like, it's your family and it's important to you. Anytime there are big changes in a family it affects all the members of that family. This means you too!

The legal picture

Separation* and **divorce*** are all about change.

But here are some things that won't change: your parents still care about you, and they still have to take care of you.

Taking care of you includes giving you affection and love, and also making decisions about where you go to school, what you can do after school and taking you to the doctor when you are sick.

If your parents were legally married, they need to go through a legal process to get a divorce. After they get the divorce, they won't be married to each other anymore.

One or both of your parents may get married again after they divorce, or they may find another person to live with. If that happens, you may become part of a new family. Even with all these changes, your parents are still your parents. They still have to look out for you until you are grown up.

Separation means your parents live in different places — a different house or apartment and sometimes in a different city, province or even a different country.

No matter where they live, they will have to work out a **parenting arrangement*** for you.

There are many ways your parents could come up with a parenting arrangement. No matter how they come up with the arrangement, it will say where you're going to live and it may spell out your schedule, who is going to pay for what, who will take you to sports practice, sign your report card or meet you off the bus and stay with you when you're sick.

Parenting arrangements are usually written down in a **parenting agreement*** or they can be part of a **court order*** made by a **judge***.

There are lots of terms used in parenting agreements and court orders. In some provinces and territories, the words **custody*** and **access*** are used. In other provinces and territories, words like *care and control*, *guardianship*, *parenting time* and *contact* are used. Each of these terms has its own meaning. In this booklet we will use the terms *custody* and *access* because those are the words used in the *Divorce Act***.

Another thing that won't change after your parents separate — they will still be responsible for paying for things you need, like food, clothing, and a place to live.

This means that your parents will have to work out a way to pay for these things now that they aren't living in the same place. The money one parent pays to your other parent to spend on taking care of you is called **child support***.

It doesn't matter if your parents were married, living together or living in two different places, there are laws in Canada to make sure that child support is paid. Sometimes a parent doesn't pay the child support they are supposed to. This can cause problems. There are special offices across Canada that will help your parents to solve that problem if it comes up. You don't have to worry about being involved in this. It is up to parents to deal with this. Try not to worry about it.

Court

Your parents may have to go to court if they can't agree on a parenting arrangement or on how much child support needs to be paid. (You probably won't have to go to court at all; most kids don't.)

To get ready for court, your parents may each hire their own lawyer to give them advice and prepare the right documents for court. Family law lawyers are people who help parents work out problems

CONTINUED ON P.12 ▶

Farah's story

Eight months after Farah was born, her dad went back up north and Farah and her mom began their lives together without him.

All that happened so long ago that Farah only remembers living with her mom. Her dad sends some money to help pay the rent on their apartment, for daycare while her mom is working, and some money for food, clothing and the other things Farah needs like dental care. Every few months, Farah sees her dad. If she's lonely for him, she can call him. She always loves it when he calls her.

But things get difficult when he doesn't send the money on time and her mom starts worrying about money. Lucky for everyone that her mom and dad work this out themselves.

about separation and divorce. These lawyers are trained to understand family law and help parents understand how family law affects them.

The court documents can be about one or many topics. For example, they may be about getting a divorce, or setting up a parenting arrangement for you and your brothers and sisters. They could also be about money or other things your parents will have to deal with now that they don't live together.

Lawyers may also help each parent prepare **affidavits*** that describe what has happened in your family. Each parent tells the story from their own point of view.

Going through the court process may take a long time. In real life, courts are not the same as courts you see on television. For example, in a small town the courtroom may be a room in a church or in a community centre. No matter what the courtroom looks like, there are certain rules that must be followed.

In most places in Canada, when your parents first go to court they will have to meet a judge. In other places the first step in the court process might be for parents to meet a family law professional. The

name used for these professionals is different across Canada. They could be called a *mediator*, *counsellor*, or *dispute resolution officer*. Whatever they're called, they will try to help your parents come to an agreement about their separation or divorce.

If your parents still can't agree after meeting with a family law professional, their lawyers will each talk to a judge. In these situations, the judge makes the final decisions about parenting arrangements, support payments and where you will live. These decisions are written in a court order. The judge's decision may not be the one you want but it will be made in your **best interests***.

In some places in Canada, when parents can't agree on parenting arrangements, a judge may decide that someone should make a recommendation about the parenting arrangement that would be in your best interests. An **assessor***, a **social worker***, a **psychologist*** or a **psychiatrist*** usually makes these recommendations. They may ask to talk to you. If they do, it will give you a chance to tell someone how you see things.

Why was the music teacher unable to open his classroom door?

Answer: Because his keys were on the piano.

REMEMBER...

- Your parents can't live together anymore, but **they still care about you**.

- Parents may have a hard time talking and listening to one another after they split up.

- **It isn't your job** to try to make them happy.

- There may be confusion and even arguments all around you during all this.

- It may seem like it's all about you, but **the real trouble is between your parents**.

Chapter Two

Coming up with a plan for you

Dad gives Randy a tough time

Every Tuesday and Thursday night during the winter, Randy's dad took him to hockey. His dad never talked very much.

But if Randy didn't do well on the ice, his dad would shoot insults at him faster than a hockey puck. Randy would feel upset.

When he got home, he couldn't wait to get out of the car. He'd listen to his dad's few words to him and then bang his bedroom door shut. Then silence. One night after this happened Randy realized that he hadn't heard his mom laugh or talk much for months.

A couple of weeks later, Randy's mom told him that she was leaving his father and that they would move in with her parents, his grandparents. He was going to miss his dad but he wouldn't miss the insults.

He packed his suitcase, wondering what would happen to Tank, his cat. His dad always forgot to feed him. So, he took the cat with him to his grandparents' house.

Randy's mom told him that she and his father would start going to something called mediation* to try and make their separation as easy as possible for Randy. For the next three months, they saw someone who does mediation. Randy went to see the mediator once to explain how he saw things and how he felt about everything that was happening.

After a few weeks of mediation, Randy's dad started taking him to hockey again. Things started going better. If Randy didn't make the goal, his father didn't call Randy names. Randy started enjoying his time with his dad again.

What's mediation?

Why are Randy's parents going to mediation? What are they hoping to do?

If your parents can't agree on anything without arguing, they may go to mediation instead of going to court or after they've been to court once. Their lawyers or the judge may suggest they do this.

Mediation may help your parents talk to each other better and make better decisions. But what about you? You probably won't go into the sessions with your parents, but you can share your feelings and wishes with them. Sometimes, arrangements will be made for you to talk with the mediator about how you see things.

If mediation doesn't work, your parents will probably have to go to court to get a judge to make important decisions.

Mom leaves dad; everyone gets help

After Joey and Tasha's mom left home suddenly, both children had trouble sleeping. Their dad called a counsellor and asked her to see the children. Their dad told the counsellor that he and his wife had split up. The counsellor agreed to see the two kids and arranged to see their dad as well. The counsellor also asked to see their mom to get the whole picture. After the counsellor met with each parent, they agreed to work with her to help figure out what sort of parenting arrangement would work best for the children.

In the sessions, the counsellor asked Joey what he liked to do after school and so he talked about his music. She asked him if he was sleeping well and if he was eating properly. "Dad's a good cook; he's the best but I miss my mom's cookies," he told her. "Every year, she made them at Christmas. What's going to happen at Christmas now? Will we see mom? I miss her."

"When I meet with your parents, I'll explain how much you miss your mom and suggest you see her very soon," the counsellor promised him.

The counsellor met with the parents soon after. She suggested that Joey

and Tasha live with their dad during the week and stay with their mom every other weekend. The parents agreed. They went to their lawyers who wrote up a **consent order*** for a judge to review. Now that there is a plan in place, Joey and Tasha are finding everything much better.

Chapter Three
Decisions, decisions, decisions

Greta's in the middle

Greta's parents never agreed on anything. Her dad liked rock music; her mom liked country. Her dad was into motorcycles; her mom was into business. And they argued about everything else too. When they split up, Greta hoped the arguments would stop.

Her parents wrote their own separation agreement. No court, no fuss. Greta's mom bought a house close to the school and Greta lived one week with her and one week with her dad.

After the separation, her dad stayed in the old house and started his own motorcycle repair shop out back. Greta loved hanging out there with him.

Then one day Greta's dad let her ride his Harley on the back roads all by herself. Excited, Greta told her mom all about it. Her mom got mad. "What kind of a parent is he anyway? You could have been killed!" she exclaimed.

Her mom phoned her lawyer. She wanted sole custody*.

This time, Greta's dad and mom met with a judge and arrangements were made for Greta to talk to a counsellor. It was good to have someone to talk to about how strict her mom was and how cool her dad was. She was tired of being in the middle of their arguments about her.

"I plan to race motorbikes when I grow up. I should live with my dad, because he'll let me do what I want. I don't want to hurt mom's feelings but she's too strict," she told the counsellor.

The counsellor had a meeting first with Greta's mom, then with her dad, and talked a lot with Greta. Finally, Greta's parents went back to see the judge. Greta's mom didn't get sole custody. Greta didn't go to live with just her dad either.

The living arrangements stayed the same as before, but the judge asked both parents to think carefully about how they were treating Greta. The judge wanted them to get help to stop putting Greta in the middle of their arguments.

After a while, Greta's parents were able to think about her feelings instead of their own all the time. Greta was relieved when she could just enjoy the time she had with her dad and her mom.

Marie is not just a babysitter

Soon after Marie's parents split up, her dad married Carole. Marie stayed with her mom. Her dad moved in with Carole and Carole's two younger children. All that first year, Marie's dad made sure he spent time with her alone, even if they just went for a walk around the neighbourhood. Marie was 10 then. "No matter what happens, I'm here for you," her dad told her.

When Marie's dad told her that he and Carole were going to have a new baby, Marie signed up for a babysitting course at school. She was so excited about having a sister at last.

After her new baby sister was born, things changed. Marie didn't get to see her dad alone anymore. "Things will get back to normal, honey. Just give us a bit of time. Eva is pretty cute, eh? She just needs some extra time right now," her dad would say.

When Marie was 12, things changed again. Whenever she went over to stay with her dad, he would suggest Carole and he needed a break from the kids. At first, Marie was pretty proud of being left alone with them. But after three months of babysitting and never spending time with her dad, she got tired of it. Her dad didn't even know that she was on the champion soccer team. There was no time to talk with him.

Marie's mom noticed that Marie no longer wanted to stay with her dad. "Maybe we can do something, honey," she told her daughter when Marie explained. Marie's mom called up her dad to talk to him about Marie's concerns. Marie's dad wanted her to be happy so he agreed to make a few changes. Marie was happy that it all worked out in the end and she could spend more time with her dad.

When you're 12 or even when you're 14, you don't get to decide where you want to live, although your thoughts and feelings will likely be considered.

As explained earlier, the judge will make the final decision in a court order. The judge must consider your best interests when making the court order.

This is nearly always a good thing because you might want things a certain way when you're eight years old, only to find out that as you grow older you want things to be different.

Your parents were two different people before they split up. They are still different people now. They may have different ideas about how to raise you. You may like one parent's rules better, but rules aren't the only things that matter. Your parents care about you even if they look at things differently. You don't have to choose between them and then feel guilty about it.

The important thing is that your family figures out where you will live and what's best for you and what works for your family. And remember, it's possible for either of your parents to ask a judge to change the court order after a while, if it would be in your best interests.

What are counsellors and assessors?

If your parents can't agree on where you will live, the judge can order an assessment. An assessment can give the judge a clearer picture of what your life is like with each parent. The idea is to make sure that the judge makes the best decision for you.

You might talk to a counsellor (or assessor) a few times. Many of them like to speak with children more than once to make sure they understand how the family works together. Maybe they'll ask you to play a game of cards or checkers or ask you to draw a picture of what your family is like.

Counsellors will write reports based on what they learn about you and your family life. They look at the whole picture and try to be fair. Here are some of the things they look at:

- **your parents' work schedules**
- **which parent helps you with school, sports or homework**
- **who looks after you when you're sick**
- **the plans your parents have made for your care**
- **the schedule that works best for all of you.**

Then, the counsellor will suggest to the judge where you should live and what your schedule for seeing your other parent should be.

Why was 6 afraid of 7?
Answer: Because 7 8 9

SPEAK OUT WHEN THINGS GO WRONG

It's tough to tell an adult that what he or she is doing is upsetting.

Talk to someone who can help you, like a grandparent or your favourite teacher.

If you feel it might be a bad idea to speak to one of your parents, pay attention to your feelings. Maybe you need to wait until you've found the right time to talk to them, or until you've found the right person to talk to.

The arrangement for your brother may not be the same as the one you have. If he is 17 and has a part-time job, his needs will be different from yours. As you get older, your arrangement may need to change again.

It can take a long time for all these meetings to take place — maybe several months. While you wait, try not to worry.

Arrangements can be changed if the situation changes. When you're older, for instance, you may not want to spend a month at your grandparents' cottage or two weeks camping with your uncle and aunt along with one of your parents. You will need time with friends or to work at a summer job.

"Our feet are sore!" agree the twins

When the twins' parents first separated, both parents wanted Monica and Reg to live with them. Their parents lived a block apart, so they decided to have them spend one night with dad, the next night with mom. Mom helped coach softball. Dad took them to art classes at the community centre. It was better than being split up like the twins in the movie, *The Parent Trap*, where each twin lives with one of the parents. Monica and Reg were close and couldn't imagine being apart. Even so, they got tired of the arrangement their parents had made.

"We've got our suitcases and our school books and our dog Hero. Our feet are really sore from carrying them all from one house to the other every day," complained nine-year old Monica. Reg agreed.

There was no time to see their friends. Monica was afraid she wouldn't be able to play softball because she often forgot where her stuff was. Would she be kicked off the team? Reg got in trouble at school when he kept losing his school books. Reg's teacher noticed that things weren't going well and spoke to Reg's dad. Then he spoke to Reg's mom. In the end, the parents agreed that spending a week with one followed by a week with the other would be easier for everyone.

Chapter Four
Living in two homes

Jacques gets used to it

It was just after his birthday when Jacques' parents separated. He hadn't even seen them arguing. "The hardest thing is being told," he says now. "You don't know what to do or what to say."

"I'd go to my dad's house and I'd miss my mom; at my mom's I missed my dad. When it first happens you are so sad, you cry. My mom asked me how I felt about it but I was too mad and too sad to answer."

That was two years ago. Jacques says it's different now. "I sort of have two of everything — two homes and different things at both places. I collect stuffed animals but I keep them all at my mom's. At my dad's house, I collect DVDs and computer games.

It's awesome having two homes and two birthday parties. I'm special in two places now!"

"Then, your parents fall in love with someone else and it's different. Dad is getting married this summer. Mom's new friend is fun; he plays cards with me and he's good. My dad's new wife isn't as much fun."

Today, Jacques finds things he likes about both homes. On bad days, he can tell you a lot about what's wrong. On the days he finds the different rules and the different houses too much, he tells himself or his younger sister, Ami, "You get used to it. Just think of the good parts."

Your parents may have an arrangement that means that you will have two homes — like thousands of other kids in Canada. It might not always be easy. And, it might take time to get used to the changes taking place. But, at times it could be fun to have two homes.

Sometimes, the separation happens when you're so young that you don't remember anything else. Jasmine is lucky. Everybody lives close to one another. She still gets to see her grandparents, aunts, uncles and the rest of her parents' families regularly. She can walk over to her dad's new house.

When both parents live near one another, kids often live with both parents but in different homes. Separation and divorce often mean that you have to move — just when you've learned your postal code!

Most kids want and need to be a part of their parents' lives and to have a place in their homes as they are growing up — whether the parents live alone, whether they remarry and have new children, or whether they go back home to live with their own parents.

REMEMBER...

No matter what the living arrangements are, your parents are always your parents.

When things work out

Jasmine lived weekdays with her mom and her mom's new partner. Her dad worked out of town. When her dad came back on the weekends, she lived with him. "It doesn't bother me because I know that I will see them both and it's been that way as long as I can remember," Jasmine explained. "I used to bring an overnight bag to school. Now, it's just easier to leave things in both places."

Even when Jasmine was young, she always knew her schedule. She liked to know where she was going to be and when she was going to be there. "When I was little, mom made me go to see my dad even though I wanted to stay with her. If she hadn't made me do that, I wouldn't know my dad, so I'm happy that she did that."

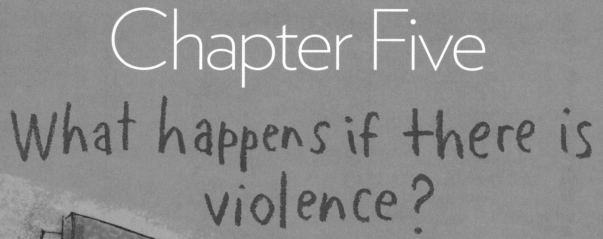

Chapter Five

What happens if there is violence?

Tommy's family finds shelter

Twelve-year-old Tommy always looked out for his two younger sisters. Being the older brother made him feel very proud. If they were okay, then he was okay too.

When Dad arrived home one night, Tommy knew he had already been drinking. Mom told Tommy to take his sisters to the neighbour's house. On his way out, Tommy could hear his dad yelling. Julie, the youngest one, began to cry and Amy was sniffling.

After about an hour, Tommy took the girls home and tucked them into bed. He sat with them until they slept. Then the argument got louder and he got really worried when it seemed like his mom might be harmed. So, he slipped outside and called "911" from the neighbour's house. His dad was gone when the police arrived. They took Tommy, his mom and his sisters to a shelter where they could be safe until his mom decided what to do. Tommy knew that things might be difficult for a while, but he was happy that he wouldn't have to worry about his mother's safety.

Sadly, Tommy isn't the only kid who lives in a home where abuse — hitting, punching, yelling and other bad things — happen.

ABUSE IS WRONG!

What does that mean? Some kinds of abuse, like beating someone up, or threatening to beat or kill someone, are against the law. Doing something physical to harm you or someone you know is physical abuse. Most forms of physical abuse are considered an assault, which is a crime in Canada.

Sexual abuse is also against the law. Even if it happens between people who are married — it is a crime. Child sexual abuse is when an adult, teenager or older child uses a young person for a sexual purpose. If someone in your family or one of their friends harms you or does something sexual to you, tell another adult you trust.

Get help. You have a right to be safe and it's ok to want to get help.

Ask someone for help — a teacher, a neighbour or a relative (a grandparent, your aunt or uncle). If the police come to your house, try talking to them.

The police will make sure no-one is hurt. They may separate your parents and take one or both of them away to cool down.

If someone is hurt, the police will likely lay charges. Then, the parent who is violent or abusive will have to go to a type of court called criminal court.

If the judge finds the abusive parent guilty, he or she might send that parent to jail or to a place that can help change his or her behaviour.

It's confusing when you have mixed feelings — like feeling scared of someone and not liking what they do, but still caring about them. Try to find someone to talk with about how you feel and who can help you work out and understand your feelings.

Some kids are hurt by their parents or by the people their parents choose to be around. Adults make bad choices sometimes. It's not your fault. It's their problem. But when violence takes place in families, it affects everyone. **Abuse is wrong. Physical and sexual abuse are against the law.**

How can the law help?

One of your parents may get an **order*** or a **peace bond*** to keep the abusive parent away from the rest of your family. This means the abusive parent might have to stay away from your home, your school or your parent's work place. These orders are legal documents, put into place to protect you and your family.

If the abusive parent disobeys the order or peace bond and tries to go into your home or anywhere else that's not allowed, the police can take the person away.

Your school and after-school program may be out of bounds too. The staff will be told about the order or the peace bond. If it would make you feel safer, you can ask the staff if they know about the order.

The idea is to protect you and your family. Efforts will be made to take care of you and to have someone there to help you. It's a tough time for everyone.

Can you still see a parent who has been abusive and violent?

Kids seem to do better if they can see both parents regularly in a safe place. If you've been allowed to see a parent every week, you will probably be able to continue. But it may take some time for visits to be arranged after the parent has been charged.

If a judge decides it is not safe for you to visit, you may not be able to see this parent for a while. This is done for your protection.

Will you have to see an abusive parent if you are afraid?

If a parent is abusive or violent and you are afraid, you may be able to have someone with you during your visit. This is called a supervised visit. If you

Why are potatoes good detectives?
Answer: Because they keep their eyes peeled.

can't handle visits with that parent, speak to someone like a counsellor or social worker who is involved in these visits. Tell them how you feel.

Your visits with a parent may be arranged so they take place in a setting away from your home like an access centre if your province or community has such centres. Centres are a safe place where a staff member stays with you during your visit with the parent. Your parents won't see each other. Rules are strict and each parent must agree to them. The visiting parent must arrive before you and your other parent. They can't leave until you are safely gone.

If you have to go to court

If you are a victim or you witnessed the violence you may have to go to court and tell the judge what happened. If this happens you will likely go to the courthouse a few days before you **testify***. Someone at the court house will explain what will happen when you talk to the judge and will give you support.

REMEMBER...

- If you or someone in your family is in immediate danger or needs help right away, call "911". You can also call your local emergency number, usually listed at the front of the phone book.

- You can ask someone to call "911" for you.

- As soon as you can, write down what happened or draw a picture of it. Speak as openly as you can about what has happened.

- Ask for help and support. You are not alone.

31

Chapter Six

Blended families, extended families, foster families and guardianship

Melody's story

Everything seemed to go well for Melody's parents until her dad got a job out of town. Then things got worse and her dad moved out. After a while her mom started to see someone else who liked Melody and her sister Violet. Melody was happy.

Melody still saw her dad whenever he came back into town to visit. Then her dad moved back to town and introduced them to his girlfriend, Jenna. Jenna was going to have a baby, and Jenna and Melody's dad were going to get married. Maybe Melody would have the baby brother she always wanted. Now, Melody had even more family and everything seemed just right to her. She spent some time with her mom and her sister Violet, who stayed with her mom; Melody had her own room at her dad's home and spent time with her new brother and Jenna.

Blended families like Melody's are made up of kids all living under the same roof but who have different moms or dads. It can be tough to be part of a blended family. The more people you put into a room together, the harder it can be for them to get along with each other without arguing, right?

Blended families are a little like that. You have six people sharing a bathroom instead of two. Different people often have different beliefs, like different foods, and have different ideas about bedtimes, school and discipline. This can make blended families complicated.

Maybe one or both of your parents has married someone who already has kids and you suddenly have a whole lot of stepsisters and stepbrothers.

No matter what kind of changes happen with your parents' living arrangements, your parents are still your parents — even if you have to share their time, affection and money with their new husband or wife and other kids.

Sometimes, parents can't take care of kids because of their drinking or drug problems or because they may have a mental illness. If living with them puts you at risk of harm, you will be moved to a safe

What kind of clothing does a house wear?

Answer: Address

Ron's grandmother takes charge

Ron's parents split up when he was a toddler. Things went okay for a while, but in the last couple of years, Ron's mother had trouble with drinking. She drank a lot and when she did, she got angry and started yelling, calling Ron names and hitting him. If Ron's grandmother was around, she would step in between Ron and his mom.

One night after Ron appeared at his grandmother's house quite late, she decided it was time for a change. She wiped away his tears and told him not to worry. Tucking him into bed that night, she promised, "I'm going to speak to your mom myself. You are going to stay with me until she gets her drinking under control. I love you."

After Ron moved in with his grandmother, he missed his mom a lot but he didn't miss the way she treated him. Things began to get better. His grand-mother helped him

with his homework and his grades improved. He made some friends and started to play baseball.

Ron's grandmother filed papers at the court asking that she be responsible for his care and schooling and giving her the right to make decisions for him. When permission was granted, she became like his parent. He decided to call her "Big Mom".

place until the situation improves. A member of your extended family like a grandparent or aunt, or a social services agency may become your guardian.

If members of your family can't take care of you, you may go to live in a foster home, or a group home where trained staff will take care of you. The idea is to keep you safe.

If a friend, teacher or any other adult sees that you are not getting proper care or that you are being abused or neglected by your parents, they must tell an outside agency. It's the law. You will only be taken into care as a last resort. This will be done to protect you. A social worker will talk to you about what's happening in your family. The social worker will also talk to your parents about your situation.

If you have extended family, like grandparents or aunts and uncles, you may move into their home. Your aunt may become your foster mom. Many kids grow up with their grandparents or aunts in the role of their parents, especially if their own parents can't take care of them.

REMEMBER...

Blended families can be tough but they can also be great.

When kids go into foster care it's because their parents can't take care of them, not because the kids have done something wrong.

Chapter Seven

When one parent moves far away

Jordan's mom Kristy wants to move

Jordan's mom Kristy was still going to school when Jordan was born. His dad Stefan was a student too. They didn't live together and Jordan only saw his dad once or twice. All of Kristy's family lived out of town. They never liked the idea of Kristy keeping Jordan without marrying his father, Stefan. So they offered no help and encouragement.

When Jordan was almost seven, things changed. Kristy's mom sent Kristy and Jordan a pair of airline tickets to Calgary asking them to visit everyone there. Jordan charmed his grandparents and his mom was over the moon about seeing her family again. Jordan's grandparents suggested to his mom, Kristy, that if she stayed in Calgary they could help her and Jordan. Both Jordan and his mom wanted to stay. Support from the family could make their lives easier. When Jordan's mom checked out a school for him, the after-school care program offered her a job.

Kristy and Jordan returned home determined to move to Calgary. The problem: when Jordan's dad found out they were considering a move, he didn't want them to go. Kristy would have to convince him to change the parenting arrangement. Could she do it?

CONTINUED ▷

To help her, Kristy visited her minister in the church and he offered to talk to Jordan's dad. After a few days, the minister called to say that mother and son were going to be able to move. He arranged for two separate lawyers to help draft a new parenting agreement and both parents signed, separately.

Kristy and Jordan moved to Calgary. They had the support of their family and life seemed better.

Jordan's dad is planning to stay in touch with Jordan by e-mail and by having Jordan live with him for part of each summer as he gets older. Jordan is looking forward to it.

Sometimes it doesn't work out quite as easily as it did for Jordan's parents. Sometimes one parent doesn't want you and the other parent to move far away. When one of them gets a new job out of town or wants to try and find a better life somewhere else, he or she will usually have to convince the other parent to allow the move.

This can be tough, especially if the parent you don't live with doesn't have a lot of money. He or she may worry about not seeing you if you move away. If your parents can't agree, both parents can go to court, give their reasons for wanting to move or not wanting the move, and let a judge decide.

The judge will consider both sides of the story and will ask some questions. For example, how hard would it be for the parent who doesn't move to find the money he or she needs to see you? How involved are you with the parent who would be staying?

REMEMBER...

You won't be able to decide for yourself whether to move. But you may have a chance to talk with someone and say what you think about it.

Chapter Eight
Nothing is perfect, but...

Pearl's birthday present

Twelve-year-old Pearl was feeling really down. Her parents had split up a few months ago. She didn't see her dad as often as she wanted and she missed his jokes. Her mom was busy working or doing stuff around the apartment. On top of all this, Pearl was having a bad time at her new school. She was sure her teachers didn't like her and some of the girls at school teased her. She tried to ignore them but she couldn't. She cried a lot instead. Everything seemed to be wrong.

Pearl decided to talk to her sister, Daisy. Daisy told Pearl that she wrote in a diary nearly every day. First, she wrote down all the horrible things that had happened or that had bugged her that day. Then, she wrote down one good thing. Daisy said it made her feel better to find that one good thing. Daisy's story helped Pearl realize that even small things can count as good things.

Soon after their talk, Daisy bought Pearl a birthday present. It was a big notebook to use as a diary. Now Pearl writes down the bad things and at least one good thing every day.

The first good thing Pearl wrote in her diary after she got it was "I'm lucky to have my sister Daisy to talk to".

All kids have good days and bad days. Sometimes when parents split up it can seem like there are lots of bad days. It can even seem like every day is a bad day.

It can help to do what Pearl did and find something good to think about. For example, Pearl realized that it was a good thing that she was able to keep her cat after the divorce. She also thought it was good that her aunt let her make cookies the last time she visited. And, she counted it as extra good that her older sister was letting her listen to some of her music. Pearl was also thinking about joining the swim team at school and thought it would give her a chance to have more fun.

NOTHING IS PERFECT BUT... SOME THINGS ARE GOOD!

If you can never think of anything good to write down and if you stay in a very sad mood for a long time (a few weeks), it is important to tell an adult you trust how down you are feeling. You may need to see a doctor for some help.

What's the difference between a train and a teacher?

Answer: The teacher says "spit your gum out" and the train says "choo choo".

ACTIVITY 1:

Write a Letter

Writing letters is a good way to deal with confusing feelings. You may want to write a letter to each of your parents expressing your feelings about their separation. You do not have to send the letters if you don't want to. Just putting your thoughts and feelings in writing may help you.

What I want to ask my Mom . . .

What I want to ask my Dad . . .

Ask Mom and Dad

If there are big changes happening in your family you probably have a lot of questions you'd like to ask your parents. You may find it helpful to make a list of questions.

ACTIVITY 3:

Draw Your Family

Try drawing a picture of your family. Or draw a picture of how your parent's separation makes you feel. You can use this space or a separate piece of paper if you need to.

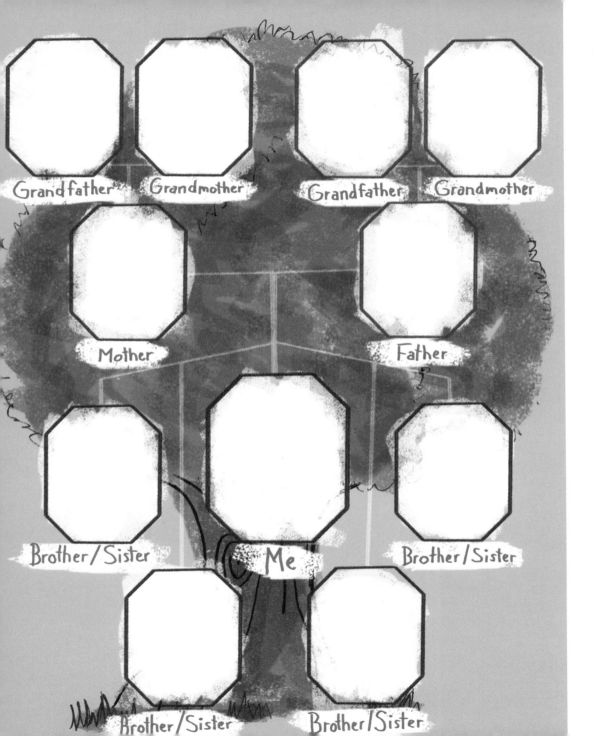

Grandfather Grandmother Grandfather Grandmother

Mother Father

Brother/Sister Me Brother/Sister

Brother/Sister Brother/Sister

ACTIVITY 4:
Draw Your Family Tree

A family tree is a drawing that lists your name and the names of other people in your family. It includes older relatives and even babies. Talk to the people in your family to get more information if you need it.

Write in the names of your family members, including stepparents or stepsisters and brothers.

If you want, you could draw or place a picture of them in the boxes or add extra boxes.

ACTIVITY 5:
Word Search

Find these words in the grid.

Custody	Kids
School	Family
Parent	Judge
Visit	Help
Coach	Pet
Time	Home

Z	V	I	S	I	T	X	R
C	Q	E	G	D	U	J	M
U	S	C	O	A	C	H	Z
S	C	F	A	M	I	L	Y
T	H	K	V	P	L	E	H
O	O	F	K	I	D	S	T
D	O	H	O	M	E	B	I
Y	L	E	T	E	P	H	M
P	A	R	E	N	T	C	E

Word Game

Unscramble the following words:

1. sohem = _____

2. yucsotd = _____

3. rapnet = _____

4. guejd = _____

Answer Key on p.57

ACTIVITY 6:

Draw a Map

If you move into a new home or if you now have two homes, it helps to know where everything is.

Try drawing a map or a picture that shows the place or places you'll be living. Include your school, the arena or community centre, the library and other places where you'll go often.

If you don't have enough space, use a separate piece of paper.

ACTIVITY 7:

Where's my Stuff?

You may have more than one home now. Try making a list of things you'll need in each home. You can also make a list of things you'll carry with you in a bag no matter which home you're going to.

These lists will help you to remember important stuff you'll want to have with you no matter where you are.

On a separate piece of paper, you can make a new list every week if you want.

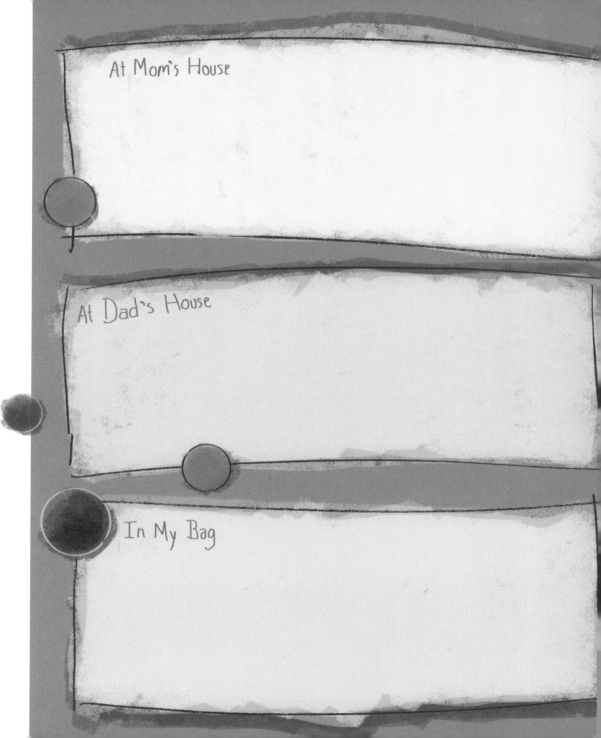

At Mom's House

At Dad's House

In My Bag

Sunday	Monday	Tuesday	Wednesday	Thursday	Friday	Saturday

ACTIVITY 8:

What's Happening?

Remembering everything can be tough. Try to keep it all straight with a calendar. Write in where you'll be living on what days and what special events are coming up with different members of the family.

For the month of

_____

CONTINUED ▶

What's Happening?

Tear-out this page and bring it with you!

For the
month of

_____

Sunday	Monday	Tuesday	Wednesday	Thursday	Friday	Saturday

My Story

ACTIVITY 10:

My Story

Why not write a story all about you? Try to use at least four words from the following list of words:

- move
- divorce
- family
- court
- love
- arguments
- school
- pets
- friends
- feelings
- separated
- brother
- sister
- teacher
- coach
- mother
- father
- aunt
- uncle
- lawyers

CONTINUED ▶

My Story

Use this page to make your story as long as you like.

My Story

Examples

- Having a pet
- Going for pizza with your big sister or brother
- Getting e-mails from a parent you don't see that often
- Riding your bike with friends
- Joining the swim team or another club
- Reading a good book from the library
- Taking the babysitting course at school when you get older to get extra money for things you want
- Thinking about things you want to do when you're grown up

My list

Hidden Treasures

Make a list of the things you like to do or things that make you feel better when you're feeling down.

Try to think of a few things that you've never thought of before.

ACTIVITY 12:
What's Next?

Try making a list of things you're looking forward to. For example, are you looking forward to a visit with relatives, or your next birthday, a trip you might be taking with family, getting together with a friend, a school you'd like to go to someday, learning to drive when you're older...

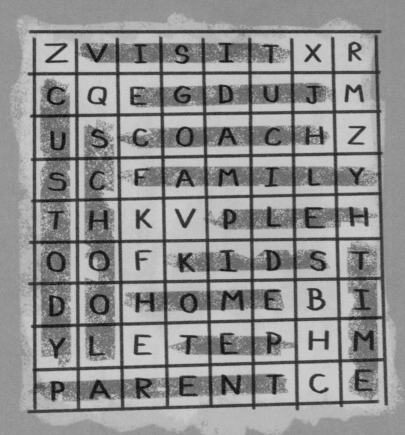

Z	V	I	S	I	T	X	R
C	Q	E	G	D	U	J	M
U	S	C	O	A	C	H	Z
S	C	F	A	M	I	L	Y
T	H	K	V	P	L	E	H
O	O	F	K	I	D	S	T
D	O	H	O	M	E	B	I
Y	L	E	T	E	P	H	M
P	A	R	E	N	T	C	E

1. sohem = ___homes___

2. yucsotd = ___custody___

3. rapnet = ___parent___

4. guejd = ___judge___

57

Appendix 2: More Information

Information for Kids

Books:

Here is a list of some good books that you might be able to find in your school or local library. They might also be available from your local bookstore.

Dinosaurs Divorce: A Guide for Changing Families. Laurene Krasny Brown and Marc Brown. Boston: Little, Brown and Company, 1986.

Divorce Is Not the End of the World: Zoe's and Evan's Coping Guide for Kids. Zoe, Evan and Ellen Sue Stern. Berkeley CA: Tricycle Press, 1997.

Family Changes: A Workbook for Families During Divorce and Separation. Kelly Carter. KidzFirst Productions. 2004. Available on the Web at http://www.kidzfirstproductions.com/, or by calling KidzFirst Productions at (902) 393-4909.

Help! A Girl's Guide to Divorce and Stepfamilies. American Girl Library. Middleton, Wisconsin: Pleasant Company, 1999.

Surviving Your Parents' Divorce: A Guide for Young Canadians. (Second Edition.) Michael G. Cochrane. Scarborough, ON: Prentice Hall, 1999.

Websites:

Here are some websites that you can look at if you have access to a computer and the Internet.

A Kids' Guide to Separation and Divorce
British Columbia Ministry of Attorney General
http://www.familieschange.ca/kids/

A Kid's Guide to Divorce
Nemours Foundation
http://kidshealth.org/kid/feeling/home_family/divorce.html

Department of Justice Canada's family violence site for youth
http://www.familyviolencehurts.gc.ca/

Family life: Separation, divorce, custody/coping
Kids Help Phone (1-800-668-6868)
http://www.kidshelpphone.ca

It's Not Your Fault
NCH
http://www.itsnotyourfault.org/

Where Do I Stand: A Child's Guide to Separation and Divorce
Ontario Ministry of the Attorney General
http://www.attorneygeneral.jus.gov.on.ca/english/family/wheredoi.asp

Your parents' separation
Educaloi
http://www.educaloi.qc.ca/en/jeunes/civil_law/other/343/

Information for Parents

Websites:

http://canada.justice.gc.ca/en/ps/pad/index.html

http://www.phac-aspc.gc.ca/publicat/mh-sm/divorce/index.html

http://www.phac-aspc.gc.ca/ncfv-cnivf/familyviolence/initiative_e.html

Appendix 3: Explanation of Terms

Access: The judge may state when and how often a parent who does not have custody can see you. You may hear people call this visitation.

Affidavits: a special written description of what has happened in your family. Usually lawyers help parents write these documents. Each parent has their own document. Each one signs their own affidavit to show that they agree with what is written down and that what is said is true. The document is then given to a judge to read.

Assessors, counsellors, social workers, psychologists or psychiatrists: Many people besides lawyers can give advice and help everyone in the family when the family is coping with all the changes that take place after a divorce. Their work is different and they are called by different names but they all listen and they all want to help.

Best interests of the child: Everyone (judges, parents, mediators, guardians, lawyers and experienced professionals) involved in deciding where you should live after your parents split up has to consider what's best for you. There are a few things that everyone usually considers when your best interests are being decided:

- The type of relationship you have with each parent before they split up
- Your physical and emotional needs
- Your parents' ability to care for you and make good decisions
- Your culture, language and religion
- Your views on the arrangement they are thinking about
- Lots of other things that are important to you!

Child protection: When parents cannot provide adequate care for their children, child protection workers may get involved to protect the children and care for their physical health as well as their emotional well being.

Child support: The money one parent gives to the other parent to help to pay for things like rent, food and clothing for a child. A support order is the document prepared by the court saying what amount must be paid for the child's food, clothing and other living expenses.

Appendix 3: Explanation of Terms

Consent order: means that your parents agreed on certain issues and had a judge sign the paper the agreement is written on.

Contact: the time that people other than your parents can spend with you. For example, your grandparents, an aunt, an uncle or maybe a very good friend of the family may want to have "contact" with you.

Court order: a decision by a judge that is written down. The order says what each person can or can't do and what they must or must not do. Court orders can be changed by going back to the judge and asking for a change, but only if there is a good reason.

Custody: a parent who has custody must take care of you and bring you up until you are an adult. Sometimes both parents have custody and that is called **joint custody***.

Divorce: parents who were married and then separated for a while (sometimes a long time) can get a divorce. When parents get divorced, a judge gives them a document that says they are not married anymore. After they get a divorce, parents can get married again.

Divorce Act: a law that tells parents, lawyers and judges what the rules are when parents get divorced.

Joint custody: this term is sometimes used when both parents have the legal responsibility to make decisions together about where you live, your school, your activities and your health. You may live mostly with one parent or you may live part of the time with each parent.

Judge: a person in court who makes decisions about parenting arrangements, child support payments, and where children will live.

Appendix 3: Explanation of Terms

Law: a collection of rules that people use to settle disagreements with one another.

Legal system: the way people use laws (rules) to make sure that everyone is treated fairly. The legal system includes the police, lawyers, judges and others.

Mediation: a way of talking about problems and exploring solutions to help solve them. A mediator is a person who runs the mediation sessions. They are a bit like hockey or baseball coaches. They try to help your parents work better as a team by giving them ways to talk with each other and make some changes.

Order (for example, civil protection, prevention, intervention, restraining, victim assistance or no-contact orders): an order is made by a judge or Justice of the Peace and tells the abuser not to contact the victim or the victim's children or to stay away from certain places such as the family home, a child's school or where a parent works.

Parenting agreement or arrangement: after they separate, your parents will have to make decisions about your care. An agreement or arrangement is often written down and usually includes things like how much time you will spend with each parent and the things each parent will do to take care of you.

Peace bond: an order made in a criminal court telling the abuser to stay away from certain places such as the family home, a child's school or where a parent works. Disobeying a peace bond is a crime.

Separation: When parents who have lived together decide they don't want to live together anymore, we say they are separated.

Sole custody: means one of your parents has legal responsibility for you and will make decisions about your school, your activities and your health.

Testify: to speak in court and tell what has happened to you or what you've seen. You may have to swear an oath on the Bible or promise that you are telling the truth and not making up stories.

Why did the jellybean go to school?
Answer: To become a smartie.

What object is king of the classroom?
Answer: The ruler.

What did one potato chip say to the other?
Answer: Shall we go for a dip?